THE STORY

OF

ARCHER ALEXANDER

FROM SLAVERY TO FREEDOM

MARCH 30, 1863

BY

WILLIAM G. ELIOT

A MEMBER OF THE WESTERN SANITARY COMMISSION
ST. LOUIS, MO.

" No sea
Swells like the bosom of a man set free:
A wilderness is rich with liberty."
WORDSWORTH

BOSTON

CUPPLES, UPHAM AND COMPANY

Old Corner Bookstore

1885

TO

MRS. JESSIE BENTON FRÉMONT,

WITHOUT WHOSE PERSONAL SYMPATHY AND ACTIVE INFLUENCE
THE WORK OF THE WESTERN SANITARY COMMISSION
COULD NOT HAVE BEEN BEGUN NOR
SUCCESSFULLY PROSECUTED,

This Little Book is Most Respectfully Inscribed

BY

HER SINCERE AND OBLIGED FRIEND,

WILLIAM GREENLEAF ELIOT.

St. Louis, Mo., Aug. 5, 1885.

CONTENTS.

PREFACE.

THE following narrative was prepared without intention of publication; but I have been led to think that it may be of use, not only as a reminiscence of the "war of secession," but as a fair presentation of slavery in the Border States for the twenty or thirty years preceding the outbreak of hostilities. I am confirmed in this view by the fact, that, on submitting the manuscript to a leading publishing-house in a Northern city, it was objected to, among other reasons, as too tame to satisfy the public taste and judgment. But, from equally intelligent parties in a city farther south, the exactly opposite criticism was made, as if a too harsh judgment of slavery and slave-holders was conveyed, so that its publication would be prejudicial to those undertaking it.

I therefore asked the opinion of several friends, who, like myself, had lived all those years under the shadow of the "peculiar institution," in one or other of the northern tier of the slave States, and who labored faithfully for its abolition, giving the best service of their lives to the cause of freedom, "possessing their souls in patience" while contending against what seemed to be an irresistible power. Their concurrence has confirmed me in the opinion, that, however feebly drawn, a true picture, so far as it goes, is given in these pages of the relation between master and slave, and of the social condition of slaveholding communities. Without claiming to be more than a plain story plainly told, it shows things as they were, and how they were regarded by intelligent and thoughtful people at the time.

Only those who lived in the border slave States during that eventful period from 1830 to 1860, can fully understand the complications and difficulties of the "irrepressible conflict," and how hard it was fully to maintain one's self-respect under the necessities of deliberate and cautious action; to speak plainly without giving such degree of offence as would prevent one from speaking at all. Yet it was in these States that the first and hardest battles for freedom were fought, and where the ground was prepared upon which the first great victories were won.

It is a subject upon which I speak with deep feeling; for I have known many cases in which those who worked with faithful and self-denying energy have been severely censured for their "temporizing, time-serving policy." Perhaps, upon mature thought, it may appear that the man who stands at safe distance from the field of battle, though he may have a better general view of the conflict, is not always the best judge of the hand-to-hand fight of those to whom the struggle is one of life or death. No city or State in the Union has greater reason to be proud of its record in the late war of secession than St. Louis and Missouri.

Gradually the mists of partial knowledge clear away; but it will be many years yet before the North and South will thoroughly understand each other, either as to the past history of slavery or the present relations of the negro and white races. Meanwhile mutual forbearance may lead to increasing mutual affection and respect.

FREEDOM'S MEMORIAL.

ABRAHAM LINCOLN. — ARCHER ALEXANDER.

"And upon this act I invoke the considerate judgment of mankind and the gracious favor of Almighty
God." — PROCLAMATION OF FREEDOM, Jan. *1, 1863.*

IN the capitol grounds at Washington, D.C.,
there is a bronze group known as "Freedom's Memorial." It represents President
Lincoln in the act of emancipating a negro
slave, who kneels at his feet to receive the
benediction, but whose hand has grasped the
chain as if in the act of breaking it, indi-
cating the historical fact that the slaves took
active part in their own deliverance.

A brief history of this memorial, taken from
the full account published at the time of its
dedication when unveiled by President U. S.
Grant, April 14, 1876, is as follows.

Soon after Mr. Lincoln's assassination, Char-
lotte Scott, an emancipated slave, brought five
dollars to her former master, Mr. William P.

Rucker, then a Union refugee from Virginia, and residing in Marietta, O. It was her first earnings as a free woman, and she begged that it might be used "to make a monument to Massa Lincoln, the best friend the colored people ever had." Mr. Rucker placed it in the hands of General T. H. C. Smith, who forwarded it to Mr. James E. Yeatman, president of the Western Sanitary Commission of St. Louis, with the following letter : —

St. Louis, April 26, 1865.

James E. Yeatman, Esq.

My Dear Sir,—A poor woman of Marietta, O., one of those made free by President Lincoln's proclamation, proposes that a monument to their dead friend be erected by the colored people of the United States. She has handed to a person in Marietta five dollars as her contribution for the purpose. Such a monument would have a history more grand and touching than any of which we have account. Would it not be well to take up this suggestion, and make it known to the freedmen?   Yours truly,

T. H. C. Smith.

The suggestion was cordially accepted, and a circular letter was published inviting all freedmen to send contributions for the purpose to the Commission in St. Louis. In response, liberal sums were received from colored soldiers under command of General J. W.

Davidson (headquarters at Natchez, Miss.), amounting to $12,150, which was soon increased from other sources to $16,242. Then came a revulsion of feeling, from various causes, after the accession of President Johnson, which checked the movement, and it could not afterwards be renewed. The amount was entirely inadequate to the accomplishment of any great work; but it was put at interest, and held with an indefinite hope of its enlargement.

In the summer of 1869, I was in Florence, Italy; and at the rooms of Thomas Ball, sculptor, I saw a group in marble which he had designed and executed immediately after President Lincoln's death. It had been done under the strong impulse of the hour, with no special end in view, except to express the magnificent act which had given new birth to his country, and for which the beloved and heroic leader had suffered martyrdom. When I told him what we were trying to do, and of our temporary failure, he said at once, with enthusiasm, that the group was at our service if it suited us, and that its cost should be only for the actual labor of reproducing it at the royal foundry in Munich, in bronze, colossal size, all of which he would gratuitously superintend himself. When told of the sum actually in hand, he said it was amply sufficient.

Accordingly I had photographs taken, and carried them home with me. The Commission thankfully adopted them, with one suggestion of change, that instead of the ideal figure of a slave wearing a liberty cap, and receiving the gift of freedom passively, as in the original marble group, the representative form of a negro should be introduced, helping to break the chain that had bound him. Mr. Ball kindly assented. Photographic pictures of ARCHER ALEXANDER, a fugitive slave, were sent to him; and in the present group his likeness, both face and figure, is as correct as that of Mr. Lincoln himself. The ideal group is thus converted into the literal truth of history without losing its artistic conception or effect. A duplicate of the group was given by Moses Kimball to the city of Boston, and stands in Park Square. It was dedicated Dec. 11, 1879, having been cast in Munich at the royal foundry, under direction of the same persons who cast the original group. But, from some cause, it is by no means equal in artistic effect to that in Washington.

The story of Archer, given in the following pages, is substantially a correct narrative of facts as learned from him, and in all the important particulars as coming under my own immediate knowledge. He was the last fugitive slave captured under civil law in Missouri.

It is written at the request of my children, for the benefit of my grandchildren, that they may know something of what slavery was, and of the negro character under its influence.

THE STORY

OF

ARCHER ALEXANDER.

CHAPTER I.

KALORAMA, ARCHER'S VIRGINIA HOME.

ABOUT twenty-five or thirty miles from Richmond, Va., in the year 1828, a family was living in the old-fashioned hospitable Virginia gentleman-farmer style, on a place of some three hundred acres, which the young folks called Kalorama, because of the beautiful outlook from the old homestead, although the name was not used except in the immediate neighborhood.

The proprietor was a man of some consequence, the Rev. Mr. Delaney, who had been, before his marriage, in active discharge of his duties as a Presbyterian minister, but had retired from all except occasional services of special interest, although still familiarly called parson or doctor by his neighbors. His wife, who brought him the property, was a lady of

great excellence, belonging to one of the best
families of the State, — a warm-hearted, devout
woman, a good manager, a faithful wife and
mother.   At the time of which I write, two
sons and three daughters were growing up, the
oldest of them eighteen years of age.   There
were ten or twelve families of slaves, number-
ing, in all, about seventy " head," old and
young.

Upon one subject Mrs. Delaney was absolutely fixed.   While believing that slavery was
a divine institution, sanctioned by scripture
from the time when " Cursed be Ham " was
spoken, down to the return of the fugitive
slave Onesimus by the apostle Paul, — subjects on which her husband had eloquently
preached, — yet she felt deeply through her
whole nature, as most of the well-born Southern women did, that there was a trust involved
for which the slave-owner was responsible to
God almost as sacredly as for his own children.
To all separation of families, therefore, except
at their own choice or as a penalty for wrong-
doing, she was firmly opposed.   It had seldom
occurred on the place, and she said it never
should occur if she could help it.   She had
also succeeded in convincing, or at least in

persuading, her husband to the same effect.
But he wavered sometimes, under the press-
ure for money, and had even suggested the
wisdom of selling off a few so as better to
provide for the remainder.

Only once, however, had he distinctly overstepped the line, and that was a signal instance. It was in the case of a man named
Aleck, a full black, forty-five years old, strong,
stalwart, intelligent; in fact, his very best
"hand." Somehow or other, this fellow had
learned to read. Nobody knew how, but
probably from the children and by chance
opportunities. A good deal of discussion
about slavery was going on at the time, which
was not very far from the Missouri compromise
days; and Aleck had got some advanced notions of which he was rather proud, talking
them out rather freely among his fellows. In
fact, "he made himself altogether too smart."
At a colored prayer-meeting he had gone so
far as to say that "by the 'Claration of 'De-
pendence all men was ekal," and that "to
trade in men and women, jess like hogs and
hosses, wasn't 'cordin' to gospel, nohow."

Of course, such talk as this would not do.
It spread among the colored folk, and the

white people began to hear of it. One of Mr.
Delaney's neighbors came to see him about it,
and after a while a committee of church-mem-
bers called upon him with a formal expostula-
tion. They urged upon him that his duty as a
Christian man required that he should send
Aleck South; "that it was not doing to his
neighbors as. he would be done by, to keep
such a mischief-maker there; that a slave in-
surrection would be the next thing."

Mr. Delaney, being a good Christian, and
believing in the divine authority for slavery,
saw the justice of what was said. He knew
that such notions as Aleck's were fanatical, and
subversive of social order. "Servants, obey
your masters," was good scripture; and he was
Greek scholar enough to know that, in the
original, "servant" meant bond-servant or
slave. So he talked with Aleck and threatened him, but it did little good. Aleck kept
at his work, but his mind was working too.
He was getting spoilt for slavery. As Deacon
Snodgrass emphatically said, "he was a demor-
alized nigger."

Still his kind mistress pleaded for him.
"Don't sell him if you can help it. Chloe
will go distracted if you do; and her boy

Archer, that his young master thinks so much of, will take it so hard!" Even she wavered, as her manner of pleading showed. She had begun to think of this sale as a necessity.

Unfortunately, Mr. Delaney was in debt. He owed a good deal of money, for the farm had not been well managed. His neighbors said he was "too easy on his niggers," for that. A suit had gone against him for fifteen hundred dollars, on which judgment was given and execution issued. He went to Richmond to arrange it and Aleck drove him down, as he had often done before; for he was a fine-looking fellow and his master was proud of him. They stopped on Grace Street, at the house of his creditor, who came to the door, praised the horses and, with an eye to business, closely scrutinized the driver. When they went in and had pledged each other, according to the hospitable notions of the times, in stiff glasses of good old whiskey, Colonel Jones poured out a glassful and took it with his own hands to Aleck, — an unusual courtesy, at which the chattel was astonished; but it gave the colonel a good opportunity of satisfying himself that the man was sound in life and limb. "Well, Aleck," he said, "your master hasn't sold you yet. I've heard talk of it." — "No, *sir*," said he. "Massa ain't a-goin' to do it, nudder. He'd most as lib sell one of his own chilluns." — "All right," said the colonel, "you just hold on to that." Aleck showed his teeth, and looked greatly pleased.

As soon as the colonel went in, Mr. Delaney began to apologize for delays, and to ask for further time. But the colonel had made up his mind, and answered abruptly, " Now, I tell you what, parson [creditors with law on their side are apt to take liberties], there ain't no use in this kind of talk. Cash is the word. But I tell you how we *can* fix it, short metre. You just give me a bill of sale for that nigger Aleck out there, and it's done. He's a sassy boy and will get you into a big scrape some day; and you'd better get shet of him, any-way, for your own good and for the good of the country. There now, parson, the way I look at it, your religion and your pocket are on the same side. What do you say? But one thing's sure : money or its equiv-a-lent I'm a-going to have, down on the nail. There ain't no two ways about that."

Mr. Delaney hesitated and pleaded. He concluded to stay over night with his consid-

erate friend. His duty seemed to him plain
enough; but his feelings rebelled, and the
thought of his wife increased the weakness.
But he prayed over it at night, and again in the
morning. His mind gradually cleared up, especially when, after breakfast, the accounts
were laid before him and the necessity of
speedy action became plain.

"What are you going to do with Aleck?"
he asked, unconsciously betraying that the de
cision was already made. "Why, now," answered the colonel with an emphatic gesture,
"that's just where it is. There's a kind of
prov-i-dence in it. Here's my neighbor, Jim
Buckner, that's making up a gang to go South,
and he wants a fancy nigger for a customer in
Charleston, and he knows Aleck and told me
to get him and he'd pay judgment *and* costs.
It's an awful big price, but he's as rich as
creases and don't care. Such a chance
wouldn't never happen again in a lifetime,
and Aleck would have a first-rate master besides. But he'll have to hold his impudent
jaw down there, *I tell you.*"

It came hard, but the bill of sale was signed,
and the debt paid. Every thing was done as
Colonel Jones said, "quiet and civil, and with-

out fuss. What's the use of hurting the boy's feelings, and your'n too, when it's got to be done?" So Aleck was sent on a pretended errand to a place near the slave-jail, taken quietly by Jim Buckner and his men, hand-cuffed, carried South the same evening, and *nobody at Kalorama ever heard of him again.* It was his death and burial.

The next day Mr. Delaney returned home, arriving late in the evening. Great was the excitement when it was known that Aleck had been sold South "to pay massa's debts," and had gone off with Buckner's gang. Poor Chloe, his wife, was dumfounded. She sat down, rocked her body backward and forward, and groaned aloud, "O Lord God, oh, dear Jesus, what has ole massa gone and done! O Lord Jesus, whar was you when he done it!" But there was no help for it, no hope for her. The next day's work must go on : so she cooked and washed as usual, heavy-hearted but silent.

"You see how it is," said Deacon Snod-grass; "these niggers don't have no feelings like white folks. Anyhow, it's only as if her old man had died. The thing happens every day, and has got to happen. It's the order of Prov-i-dence."

Mrs. Delaney was deeply grieved. The young master, Thomas, took it hardest at first, and said right out, "it was a damned shame." But his father rebuked his profanity, and explained the case to him as one of unavoidable Christian duty. Aleck's son Archer was too young to understand it; but he kept close to his mother, who, after that, never liked to lose sight of him. The neighbors generally said it was a good thing; "that Delaney's niggers had got too uppish, and would now be brought down a peg. It was high time for an example."

Two years had already passed since that "taking down a peg" had occurred; but, on the whole, things had not improved. The farm kept deteriorating in value, worn out by exhausting crops of corn and tobacco. One of the hands ran away and escaped. Another who tried it, with his wife and child, was caught and brought back; but they had suffered so much from exposure and in the struggle with their captors, *who had an unmanageable dog with them*, that they were never of much account afterwards. From such experience the rest could not fail to learn the wisdom of submission and contentment. Yet a spirit of

uneasiness prevailed, so unreasoning is the
African mind. The increasing probability of
being sold South, and the difficulty of running
away, did not seem to have a soothing influence.

In 1831 Mr. Delaney died suddenly, leaving no will and many debts. The estate was
administered upon, and about one-half the
land, with three or four families of slaves, were
sold to pay the pressing debts. The rest of
the property was divided, under the law, among
the widow and children. In this division
Chloe fell to the widow's share; her boy
Aicher, now eighteen years old, to the "young
master," Mrs. Delaney's oldest son. But
Chloe, Aleck's "widow," had run down very
sadly. It really seemed almost as if she had
had feelings like white people, and Aleck's
being sold South was in some way or other
very different to her from a divine dispensa-
tion of bereavement. A clergyman talked
with her; but when he said, "The Lord gave,
and the Lord hath taken away; blessed be the
name of the Lord," — she said with sobs, "O
Lord, massa! please don't talk dat way! I
can't see it, nohow!" She was no longer
cheerful and full of jokes, but stolid and heavy-

hearted, taking no interest in any thing except her boy Archie. It was not long before she had to lose him too, though not by death.

Mrs. Delaney's eldest son, Thomas, whom Chloe had nursed in his infancy, made up his mind to emigrate to Missouri, the new land of promise in the West. His mother and the rest of the family would stay in the old place. He quietly made all his arrangements, sent part of his valuables forward to Guyandotte to wait for him there, and when quite ready, one day after dinner, told Archer, his foster-brother, to saddle up the horses and get ready for a start, so as to make twenty miles before night set in.

Of course, the old tradition of not separating families had been broken up, in the settlement of the estate. The law is no respecter of persons or feelings. It allows little place for sentiment, and the family plate is worth the silver in it; no more. Every thing had been appraised at its value, slaves included; and, if families could not be kept together, it was nobody's fault. They were sold under the hammer, "to the best advantage."

It is a great mistake to suppose that the chief hardships of slavery consisted in acts of

severity or cruelty. Such did frequently occur,
for irresponsible power over an inferior race is
sure to result in its abuse ; but they were the
comparatively rare exceptions, and in no part
of the South were they the rule. The vast
majority of slave-owners ameliorated the condition of slavery; that is, so far as they con-
veniently could, consistently with their own
interests, the maintenance of subordination,
and a friendly regard to the rights of their
neighbors. They looked carefully after the
comfort of their "families" up to a certain
point, treated them with humanity and sometimes with indulgence and tenderness. Never-
theless they were "chattels" (Anglice, "cattle "), — in the eye of the law, property subject
to seizure and sale. The exigencies of debt,
so common in the unthrifty Southern management; the death of the owner, and consequent
necessity of dividing the estate; the commission of faults of impudence or petty criminal-
ity, to say nothing of the whims and caprices
of the master or mistress, — all were common
and lawful causes of trouble. Over the best
and most pampered slave the sword of uncertainty always hung, suspended by an invisible
hair; from which it came to pass, that, under

the best of circumstances, the best condition
of slavery was worse than the worst condition
of freedom. The blacks are a docile and
easily controlled race. Subordination does
not come hard to them. But at this moment, —
twenty years after they have had the trial of
freedom, trammelled as it has been by not a
few hardships and social oppressions, and by
greater cruelties in some sections than slavery
itself witnessed, — I doubt if a man or woman
could be found who would exchange freedom,
such as it is, for the old relation under the
best master that ever lived.

Six months after Archer's going, Chloe, his
mother, died. There was no special disease;
but "she kind-a fell off," as the colored people expressed it. "She didn't take no hand
in nothin', like she used to;" did her work
faithfully, but "seemed to be a thinkin' about
somethin', and *prayed powerful.*" Her kind-
hearted mistress said she never got over
Aleck's being sold South, and just grieved
herself to death; but Deacon Snodgrass, who
"understood niggers," said that she was "the
obstinatist nigger-wench he ever knew."

CHAPTER II.

THE DEPARTURE.

THE sudden bustle of the final getting-ready stirred up the household. The family partings were made between Mrs. Delaney and her son. Very sad and bitter they were; but the old lady knew it was best for Thomas, and so she gave him her blessing and was resigned. Then "young massa" went out and shook hands with all the people, every one of whom loved him, for he had been kind to all of them. He gave them some trifling gratuities, and told them to behave themselves first-rate till he came back. Then, last of all, he looked for his old nurse Chloe, who was at the door of her cabin, and shook hands with her, and promised to take good care of Archie, and to fetch him back some day to see her. He gave her a new calico gown, for which she "thanked him kindly." In fact, she had no hard feelings towards him. He was only doing what he had a right to do; and "mebby it's the best thing for the boy; and de good Lord, he knows best what's good for all on us." She seemed to feel very much as Mrs. Delaney did, though of course no one would have ventured to make so absurd a comparison between a slave woman and her lady mistress. But there she stood; and, when her young master turned away, the tears were running down her cheeks.

As for Archie, boylike, he was full of excitement. He ran up to kiss his mammy, told her he was going to ride "Shirley," the old master's favorite horse, and Master Thomas was to ride "Major," and they were most ready to start. She tried to look pleased, but the tears kept coming. "Well, go way, chile; come back to see de ole place ef you kin. Mebby you'll fine me here." She sat down on the stoop, and he was off in a minute on a run.

A MOTHER'S LOVE.

Forty-eight years after that day, Archer himself told me of it. He was then nearly seventy years old, failing very fast, about three months before he died. I had often talked with him about his old home; but he had said almost nothing about his mother, until one day, as he was half-working on my grass-plot

with his sickle, I asked him if he remembered
her. "Yes, sir," he answered very slowly and
solemnly, first looking at me, and then higher
up, with his face raised. "Yes, sir, I remem-
bers her like yesterday. Seems like I never
forgets her, nohow. 'Specially when trouble
comes, and I've had a heap of that, — thank
the Lord, — seems like she allays come to me
— not close up to me, but jess like she was
when I seed her the last time; and she's allays
a-prayin' for me. That's what keeps me up."

There was something peculiar in his manner, for to the pious negro there are no reali-
ties like those of faith; and I asked him to tell
me more about it. He hesitated a moment,
and then said, "Yes, sir, I think I kin. I can't
allays talk about it, but it 'pears like it would
do me good now." He sat down on his wheel-
barrow, while I stood by him, under the shade
of a tree that he had helped me to plant ten
years before.

"You see, sir, after ole Mr. Delaney died,
and the family was all broke up, like what I
was tellin' you one day, the place wasn't big
enough to keep all on us; and young Mr.
Thomas he thote to come West, and he was
bound to take me, 'cause he liked me, and I

liked him ; and I belonged to him, anyhow, as a part of his sheer. Well, one day, on a sud-dent-like, he up and quit. He said good-by to eberybody, and I kissed my mammy, and was most crazy with 'citement 'kase Massa Tom had chose me to go along wid him, and to ride his favorite hoss 'Shirley;' and I didn't know what a big fool I was.

"I leff my mammy — that ar was Chloe, the ole missus' favorite cook — a-settin' on the door-step, and I didn't seem to keer no more about it than ef I was goin' away for a week. But she keered. Then, when we went down to the gate that one of the boys was thar to open, suthin' came inside of me, right here [laying his hand on his breast], and said to me, ' Archie, you're leaving your mother for good. You won't neber see her no mo'.' Then I turned round to see whar she was. And thar she stood, front of her own white-washed cabin, whar I was born; and both her hands was raised up, this way; and she was lookin' up, and the sun shined on her, and I could see her face plain, and it looked bright-like round her head, and I knowed she was a-prayin' for me. I knowed it jess as well as ef I heerd it. I kep' looking so long that Massa Tom got a

good bit away; and he turned and spoke up
sharplike, 'Come, hurry up thar! What you
lookin' at thar like a stuck pig?' So I turns
round and rode up to him, but my 'citement
was all gone. 'Peared like I weighed twice as
much on the hoss as I did before, and I
could'nt say nuthin'. 'Why, what's up,
Archie?' young massa said: 'have you seen
a ghost?'—'No, sir, I ain't,' I said to him;
'but I seen my mammy, and she was a-prayin'
for me.'—'Well,' said he, keerless-like, 'that's
all right. Your mother will pray for you, and
mine will pray for me.'—'Yes, Massa Tom,
that's so.'

"You see, sir, my young massa was mighty
good to me. He knowed I felt bad, and
wanted to keep my heart up. But I couldn't
do it, nohow. That night we stopped at
Jake Appler's tavern, and I dreamed all night
of my pore ole mammy. But arter that I
didn't think hardly no mo' about it. I was
drefful busy all the time, and when we got to
the river at Guyandotte, and on the boat, there
was a heap to see. But at Louisville, whar we
stopped two days, I seed her agin."

He paused for a moment as if to collect his
thoughts. He was evidently telling what was
to him literal and sacred truth.

"Massa Tom, he leff me waitin' for him in a bar-room, — you see he trusted me anywhar, — and some men thar was mighty civil, and give me a drink, and got me to laughin', and I was goin' it strong. All at once sumfin come over me. I looked out of the winder (it was jess beginnin' to be darkish), and thar, plain as I see you — thar she was, away off, stanin' front of her whitewash door, de light shinin' on her face and all aroun' her, and her hands up, a-prayin' for me, — seemed like I heerd her, — 'Lord Jesus, save my boy.' I sot down the glass. 'Gentle*men*, 'skuse me. I speck my massa's callin' for me, and I'se bound to go.' When I tole Massa Tom how kind them men was to me, he was orful mad. He said they was *dealers*, the damn rascals, and, ef they had only got you drunk, they'd 'ducted you in no time, and sole you South. But I didn't tell him it was my mammy that saved me." It is impossible to express the tenderness with which he said this.

"Well, sir, it was a long time after that afore I thote serious about any thing; for, arter we got to St. Louis, I was worked in the brick-yard, and nothing much went wrong wid me. But there come round thar a 'vival Metherdus preacher, and I went to hear him. He talked mighty strong, persuadin' to come to Jesus; but somehow it didn't 'press me much. He called for them as wanted to be prayed for to come forrard, but I got up to go home. Jess then, seemed like I heerd my mammy a-prayin', 'Lord Jesus, don't let him go!' Shore enough, right out in the dark night I seed her, plain as day, her hands like they was befo', prayin' for me. I jess give in and went straight up to the altar, and afore the week was gone I found Jesus; and, bless the Lord, I'se stuck to him ever sense. But it was my mammy that done it.

"It's a long time ago, and I haven't seen her plain till lately; but now, ebery night mose, she comes in my sleep, allays a-prayin' for me, and her looks is pleasant. She's dead long ago, and gone to glory. I never heerd nuthin' certain about it; but, sir, I'm thinkin' I sha'n't be here long now. Please the Lord, she's waitin' for me. I'se ready to go.

"Mebby, sir, you think this is all fool talk. I'm a pore ignerant man, ef I is free, thank the Lord! Kin you tell me, sir, ef you please, was it my mammy all this time, shore enough? Or is I 'ceivin' mysef? I see you don't make fun of me, and you's the fust one I ever tole it all to."

"No, Archer," I said, "I don't feel like laughing. I could never laugh at a man for loving his mother. What you saw I don't know; but one thing is sure, that it is your mother's love, and your memory of her, that has saved you."

"Thank you, sir; that comforts me and 'courages me. We don't know much, nohow, but I'll go along steadier for what you say. I'm gettin' powerful weak, and my mammy is a-waitin' for me."

I left him sitting there. It was his last day of work.

All of this may seem trivial, childlike, superstitious, but it is illustrative of the uneducated negro character, when sincere piety has taken possession of it. The strength and weakness of the African nature as seen in American slavery came from its implicitness of faith. We may smile at it, but from it often came the most excellent results. I have given the narrative in this place, because it furnishes the key to Archer's subsequent history, and shows the spirit of love and faith in which he lived. A childlike or even childish faith may give birth to the most manly character. Unbelief, however learned, is barren of such fruit.

CHAPTER III.

THE life of Archer for the next thirty years varied but little in its general tenor from that of the majority of well-behaved slaves held in bondage by kind masters. The treatment of slaves in Missouri was perhaps exceptionally humane. All cruelty or "unnecessary" severity was frowned upon by the whole community. The general feeling was against it.

Archer's young master, Mr. Thomas Delaney, was not only kind and considerate, but he was personally attached to his servant, who was nursed at the same breast, and had been his constant playmate in boyhood. He was also under promise to his own mother and to Archer's mother to do what was right by the boy.

For three or four years, while in St. Louis, Archer was hired out and worked in a brickyard (Letcher & Bobbs), at the end of which time Mr. Delaney bought a farm in the western part of St. Charles County, and moved there to live. Soon after being settled in his new home, he married a lady from Louisiana, who brought him some considerable property. About the same time, Archer "took up" with a likely colored woman named Louisa, and was regularly married to her with religious ceremony, according to slavery usage in well-regulated Christian families. Louisa belonged to a thrifty farmer named Hollman, in the near neighborhood, on the border of St. Charles and Warren Counties. This gentleman had learned what a faithful fellow Archer was, and when, a few years later, Mr. Delaney, who was any thing but thrifty, concluded to move South, where his wife's property was, he was easily induced to sell Archer at a high price to his neighbor, particularly as neither of them was willing to separate man and wife, to whom several children had now been born. In fact, this was Mr. Delaney's chief reason for selling Archer, to whom he was more and more attached. It happened, too, that Mrs. Delaney wanted the money, and took pains to convince her husband that it would be wrong to separate the family, and that "Archer would be sure to run away if they did." So, from these mixed motives, the sale took place ; and the slave husband and wife were comfortably settled in their cabin, with a growing family of children, for more than twenty happy years. Their master was a religious and humane man. He looked upon slavery as a patriarchal institution, sanctioned by divine law, in no way inconsistent with the republican principles of a free country, and that it was the only condition for which the colored race were providentially fitted. A strange creed, — but if all slave-owners had put it in practice as kindly as he did, we might possibly in some small degree understand the delusion. Even on his place, however, the bad behavior of husband or wife, of parent or child, was sometimes punished by "sending the offender away," which was a virtual decree of divorce, and so recognized, not only by usage, but by the deliberate decree of the churches.[1]

For Archer no such suffering was in store. He was a faithful man, and was trusted accordingly. As the trust was increased, so was the trustworthiness. He became a sort of overseer, and, as he said, "Mr. Hollman trusted me every way, and I couldn't do no other than what was right." Some of his children behaved badly, being over-indulged, and were "sent

1 See Appendix I.

away ; " but he didn't seem to blame his master for it. The heart learns to bear inevitable burdens.

But in all this time the political and social condition of Missouri was gradually and rapidly changing. The boldly proclaimed Free-Soil doctrines of Thomas H. Benton were taking possession of the public mind. As early as 1854, Francis P. Blair, jun., to whom the whole nation owes a debt of gratitude which has never been adequately acknowledged, stood up in the General Assembly at Jefferson City, avowing himself a disciple of that school. He plainly said (although it seemed at the time like taking his life in his hand to say it) "that all the best interests of Missouri demanded the extinction of slavery; that, even if it could be defended as right and profitable in States farther south, it was simply a blight and a curse here." As time passed on, the truth of such ideas appeared more plainly, and the unprofitableness if not the wrong of slavery was more generally admitted.

The slaves themselves, or the more intelligent of them, began to feel that there was something in the air affecting their relation with their masters, and that in some way or other it might soon be changed altogether. Many of them were removed, either with their masters or by being sold to the Southern States. Many ran away and found secure refuge in the neighboring Free States and Territories. Even on the best-managed farms a sense of uneasiness began to prevail, and the uncertainty of slave property to be felt. The slaves felt it no less than their masters.

Then came the Kansas conflict, the great struggle for the extension or restriction of slave territory, the turning-point of true Republican progress, by which the whole country was thrown into a paroxysm of excitement. The terrible complication of affairs as existing in Missouri, especially on its western borders, was not then, and is not yet, understood in the Eastern States. Those on the right side, for freedom and humanity, were guilty of many outrageous acts of wrong. The slavery advocates thereby found excuses for themselves, and redoubled their atrocities.

John Brown of Ossawatomie, with his heroic ideas of freedom and philanthropy, half blinded by the wrongs he had suffered, forgot, he and his followers, that to do evil that good may come is under Christian law a forbidden policy.

He said he would "fight the Devil with fire," and did so; but that is not the law of the Lord Jesus, though God may sometimes overrule it for good.

A true history of that fierce struggle will probably never be written. There were no impartial judges, no unprejudiced witnesses, to observe or record the facts. Right-minded men could hardly tell where the lines of right and wrong crossed each other. Living in St. Louis the whole time and long before, and knowing many of those engaged in the strife on either side, I thought I saw both sides as they really were, but, in truth, I saw neither. The complications of action and motive, both right and wrong, were past finding out. One thing, however, is sure: that the right prevailed at last. Thank God for that.

But it will be readily understood that in the progress of a strife that affected, for good or ill, all social interests, every household would be disturbed. The more intelligent negroes, both free and slave, were pretty well informed as to the tendency of public thought, and, when the die was cast by the election of Lincoln, a vague but strong hope was everywhere spreading that the day of freedom was at hand.

At Archer's home, in St. Charles County,
close by St. Louis, the centre of Free-Soil
strength, the current of thought circulated
freely. Trusted as he was, he heard from day
to day, from those who talked freely in his presence, what was going on. He heard it without
full comprehension, but with a growing conviction that freedom was his rightful inheritance,
under the law of Christ. He may have inherited
something of that feeling from his father Aleck,
the story of whose hard fate he well remembered. In fact, he had remained contented in
the condition of slavery more from religious
motives, as being the will of God, than from
consent to human law. At my first acquaintance with him I could not help seeing this.
He spoke of his former employer as *Mr.* Hollman, not master, and never used the latter term
at any subsequent time, except when speaking
of his Virginia boyhood life. He had pretty
well outgrown the spirit of bondage, and was
already entered upon that of freedom. He
was quite prepared to do his part in breaking
his chains.

Mr. Hollman was " a Union man with
slavery," not without it. He was what afterwards came to be called a " Haystack Seces-

sionist," staying at home with his property, but sympathizing with the South and helping it whenever he could without too great risk. After Camp Jackson, in St. Louis, was broken up (10th of May, 1861), and Union troops were on their way to Jefferson City, he joined a band to cut down or burn bridges and encumber the roads, to intercept or delay their progress. Archer knew of this, and began to make up his mind that the time for action was near; but more than a year passed before it came.

In the month of February, 1863, he learned that a party of men had sawed the timbers of a bridge in that neighborhood, over which some companies of Union troops were to pass, with view to their destruction. At night he walked five miles to the house of a well-known Union man, through whom the intelligence and warning were conveyed to the Union troops, who repaired the bridge before crossing it.

CHAPTER IV.

THE ESCAPE.

IN some way the suspicion arose that Archer was the "traitor." Mr. Hollman did not believe it, but promised to bring Archer before the committee for examination. He threatened Archer, and commanded him to keep in the house unless he wanted to be shot, and the poor fellow saw plainly what was coming. He was in a terrible dilemma, — without money, without arms, with nobody to consult, afraid to speak even to his own wife, in momentary danger of being killed. What could he do?

In the middle of the night he got up quietly from his bed, and went out into the open air, cold and cheerless in the wintry wind, "to ask the good Lord what this pore forsaken nigger should do." He walked on for nearly a mile; and then turned to retrace his steps. Then, to use his own words, "The Lord he answered me! It came on me like a flash of lightnin'. *I felt like I was stripped.* Suthin' said inside of me, 'What you goin' back for, like a fool idgyut, to be shot or whipt to death like those fellers whipt Sam last week? Go for your freedom, ef you dies for it!'"

So he held on his way right southward, until he had crossed the river at early daylight, and then lay down for a short sleep in the woods. Soon after starting again, he fell in with a party of six or eight negro men, who, like himself, were making for freedom; but at noon they were overtaken by a band of mounted pursuers, who compelled them to go back as runaways, to a tavern on the south bank of the Missouri, which they reached before dark. There the party concluded to stay over night. They were in high glee, for there was "a big prize" offered for the runaways, whom they stowed safely in a room up stairs, gave them cornbread and bacon and some bad whiskey, and told them to take it easy and no harm would come to them. Then they went themselves into the bar-room for a grand carouse, which they kept up till midnight. The negroes were completely disheartened. They eat their cornbread and bacon and drank all the whiskey, and, laying themselves down on the floor, were soon fast asleep.

All except Archer. He sat down on a box
by the window to think. He had noticed that
box when he first came into the room, for a
strong cord was wrapped round it several times,
and he thought it might help him to escape.
So he unwrapped it, and took the cover off the
box, which was filled with wood. He found a
knot-hole, through which he put one end of the
rope, and tied it to a stick so as to keep it from
slipping when he should let himself down by
it, if he got the chance. Then he knelt down
and said his prayers, and "begun to have some
hope." He had drunk no whiskey, but had eat
all he could, and put "a chunk of cornbread"
in his pocket.

As soon as it was all quiet down stairs, — " I
thote they would never be done swarin' and
singin', " — he softly got up and examined the
windows. They were nailed down tight; but
fortunately he had a small claw-hammer in his
pocket, — " I allays had it with me, and it was
mighty good luck," — and without any noise he
drew the nails carefully. It was a bright moonlight night, clear and fresh, and he could see
perfectly to do his work. Waiting a few minutes to be sure that all was quiet, he raised
the window "soft and easy." "Then," to use

his own words, " I puts my head fru de winder
to see what kind of a chance I had. The
moon it was shinin' bright as day, and, ef you'd
believe me, thar was the biggest kind of a dawg
a-walkin' backerd and forrerd, and he jess
looked up at me, a-kind o' winkin', as ef he said,
' *No, you don't!* ' I had thote them slave-ketchers had been mighty keerless, leavin' us up thar
without a watch, but now I onerstood it all.
I sot down on the box jess flustrated. I hadn't
no more hope, not a mite. Sure enough, the
Lord had done forsook me. I leaned my head
down on the winder-sill and cried like a chile.
How long it was I don't know, but I 'speck I
cried myself asleep, for when I looked up again
I felt fresher and more cheery-like. The
moon had gone down behind the trees, and the
shadders was black, but over to the east I
seed the fust little show of daylight. I put my
head out agin, and thar was the dawg settin'
down and watchin' of me. He knowed his
business sure. There didn't seem no way out
of it, nohow."

But a way did open itself most unexpectedly,
in accord with the nature of dog and of man ; for
suddenly he heard off in the woods, three or four
hundred yards away, the barking of a coon.

The dog heard it too, and that was too much
even for his faithfulness. To tree that coon
was his first and most earnest vocation, and off
he started as fast as his legs would carry him.
"Now's my chance," said Archer to himself :
"the Lord pints the way." He took strong hold
of the rope, dropped himself down gently to
the ground. The box was heavy, but so was
Archer; and it "wobbled," and when he let go it
gave a "ker-thump" on the floor.

He knew that this must wake up the slave-
catchers, and he slipped quickly round the corner of the house in the shadow of it, and waited.
Sure enough, the door opened and one of the
men came out. He looked up at the window
and saw the rope hanging down. Then he
heard the dog over in the woods, and called
out to his mates, "The niggers have got away,
and the dog is after them!" They all rushed
out, not very clear-headed after their night's
carouse, and, without stopping to look, "made
tracks for the timber." When Archer saw
this, negro-like, he "couldn't help larfin, though
skeered to death, to see them men fooled so
bad by their own dawg." But he wasted no
time, and, keeping the house between him and
them, he ran "like a skeered dawg," until he

was well out of sight before they could have
discovered their mistake. · At about a half-
mile's distance he came to some "slashes,
where it was all wet and mashy," and he "put
right through the swamp so as to kill the scent."
He was at that time close to the St. Louis
road; but it was getting light, so that he could
see the tavern that he had left, and he was
afraid to keep on. He found a place where
the bushes were thick, and lay down among
them so as to be completely concealed. " Ef
you'd believe it," he said, "I dropt right off
asleep like a chile in its cradle. I was jess
tired out and mose dead."

His hiding-place was well chosen, for when
he waked, about ten o'clock, he peeped through
the bushes and saw the "slave-ketchers and
their gang" on their way from the tavern to
the ferry-boat. They had failed or had not
attempted to trace him. Still he was afraid
to start out on the open road, for some of the
men might be around, watching for him; and,
although he was "drefful hungry," he "kept
right thar until dark came." "As soon as it
was clear dark I got a-goin', and walked steady
all night along the road, till I come to whar
the houses begin outside of St. Louis. The

daylight was jess comin' on, and I didn't know
what to do nor whar to go, but jess loafed
along until some how or another I struck that
market-house close to Bumont Street. I asked
the butcher-man, that was a Dutchman, for a
job. He asked me ef I was a runaway nigger.
I tole him I 'speck so. He larfed and said,
'You wait thar and I'll give you a chance.' In
about an hour he call me and said thar was a
lady who wanted me to take her basket home.
I looked at the lady, and she seemed so kind
and pleasant that I knowed she wouldn't be
hard on a poor feller like me ; and then when
she spoke up and said, 'Uncle, if you will take
this basket home for me, it isn't far, I'll give
you a dime and a good breakfast,' it seemed
like a angel was a-callin' of me." Nor was he
far from right.

CHAPTER V.

THE CAPTURE.

IN the month of February, 1863, I was living with my family at Beaumont Place, in what was then the western suburbs of St. Louis. It was a lovely spot, containing about four acres, with a grove of forest-trees, a small but choice orchard, a vegetable-garden and lawn, with an old-fashioned one-story farmhouse upon it. There were long porches, a wide hall, and rambling outhouses, that made the homestead altogether capacious enough for a large family. In the months of April and May, with trees in full glory, it seemed like a sort of paradise, in contrast with the noisy and disturbed city. It had formerly been occupied by one of my oldest and dearest friends, Dr. William Beaumont of the United States army, a man of great skill and wide celebrity, whose death I do not yet cease to mourn. Previously to his occupancy, it was the residence of Gov. Hamilton Gamble, by whom the house was built.

We had ourselves moved there in May, 1861, just after the war of the Rebellion had broken out. In St. Louis it was indeed a civil war, a fratricidal strife. I well remember when the news came that the United States ship " Star of the West " had been fired upon, and Fort Sumter attacked by Beauregard (I am glad that it is not an American name), in Charleston harbor, what intense excitement and animosities were aroused. The nearest neighbors were set against each other, and brothers against brothers. Parents and children, husband and wife, were enlisted on different sides. I had taken my stand firmly and plainly, and, in my peaceful way, had enlisted for the war. After having done my poor best to prevent it, there was no alternative but to fight it through. Many of our friends advised us not to go outside of the city to live, as being unsafe in such a disturbed condition of affairs : and before we had been in our new home many days we were half of that opinion ourselves; for Camp Jackson, organized to favor State secession, was but a half-mile from us, and, when broken up by General Lyon and the Home Guards, the rifle-bullets came close to our fences. Afterwards the large buildings known as " Uhrig's Cave " were occupied by volunteer troops under General B. Gratz Brown. In their clumsy manœuvres and musketry discharges, the balls whistled across our grounds to the no inconsiderable danger and discomfort of the family. Yet through all the four years of strife I walked to and from the city at all hours of day and night, generally alone, without the slightest annoyance or cause of fear.

The place was in a sadly neglected condition when we went there; and all we could do in the first years was to clean up the grounds, trim the trees, and make things generally look as if somebody lived there. But at the end of the second year, my boys and myself thought we must have a garden and other improvements, which prompted us to the extravagance of a man-servant, if we could find one at low wages. Accordingly, when my wife went to market one morning, at the corner of Jefferson Avenue and Market Street, she inquired of the butcher if he knew of any colored man who wanted such a place. He answered, "Yes, madam, I think I do. That boy standing there came to-day, about two hours ago, and seems clever and willing. It would be charity to employ him. I'll tell him to take your basket to your house, and you can see what you think of him." So he called the "boy," being a man of full fifty years, who came forward with an uneasy, timid look, but was ready enough to take the basket and go with the lady. She spoke to him once or twice on the way, and he gradually got courage as he looked at her, as well he might. When they were inside the gate, he glanced round with a brightening face and said, " Did I onerstand, madam, that you is wanting a man to take keer of this place ? " She answered, " Yes, can you tell me of one ? " He looked at her earnestly, with the peculiar expression of the negro face, keeping his eyes steadily upon her while his head rolled round, and answered beseechingly, " I should like sech a place oncommon well myself, ef you please, madam, and I'd serve you faithful." Following the lady to the house, he waited in one of the outbuildings, where my son Thomas went to see him and find out what he could do.

" Take care of horse and cow ? " — " Yes, sir." — " Keep the grass and trees in good order, and lay out a garden ? " — " Yes, sir, I kin."— " Can you plough ? " — " Plough, sir ! why, my name's for ploughin'. In fac', sir, I'se a farm hand, and there ain't nothin' ' bout a farm that I don't know, and ef your father tries me he'll be satisfied sure."

As to who he was and where he came from, he was rather shy. His name was " Aleck, and he didn't edzackly belong to the city," — that was all he would say. He was shown into the kitchen, where the good-natured Irish cook put before him, as she said, enough breakfast for three men, but he eagerly eat it all. Poor fellow! he seemed half famished.

In about half an hour I went down to see what I could make of him. He studied my face very closely, keeping all expression out of his own, for several minutes ; but by the instinctive perception which the negro seems to have, just as the dog has it, he saw that I was not likely to betray him, and soon opened his mind more freely. He had come — carefully avoiding the word " runaway " — from his old home up in the State, because of some disturbance there. He left without telling anybody where he was going. He was sometimes called Aleck, but his right name was Archer Alexander. All he wanted was a quiet place to work. He would take just what wages I pleased, and he " jess wanted to keep close to his self."

Evidently a fugitive slave, one of the thou-

sands who, with or without reason, had taken
their chance for freedom. The events of the
previous years in Missouri had shaken society
to its centre. More than sixty battles or skir-
mishes had taken place in the State beside local
strifes, resulting in over five thousand killed and
wounded, so that the bitterness of war was
everywhere felt. On every farm and in every
household the possibility of emancipation was
discussed, and its almost certainty began to appear. General Frémont's proclamation of freedom to all slaves of rebel masters, although
unfortunately and unwisely revoked by President Lincoln, only foreshadowed what was coming. Martial law, extended over the State,
practically placed all fugitive slaves under
protection of the military authorities. No one
but a loyal master could successfully reclaim a
fugitive, and then only under regular civil process. Such was the condition of things in the
spring of 1863, — unsettled, revolutionary, with
nothing clearly defined, neither slave nor slave-
holder having any rights which they felt bound
mutually to respect. But the whole tendency
was towards freedom, and all thoughtful persons
saw that it must there reasonably end.

When the fugitive Archer had disclosed the

facts, therefore, I was not a little puzzled what to do. He said his master was "the worst kind of Secesh," and had helped to burn down bridges with his own hands to stop Union troops, though he had never enlisted; but I had only his word for it. I had always been an advocate for obedience to law, and prided myself upon it, though an equal advocate for freedom. When the fugitive-slave law had been enacted by Congress, that great judicial blindness of the South, I had said openly in the pulpit that I, for one, could not obey it, but should be ready to bear the penalty of paying the price of the non-surrendered slave or of the adjudged imprisonment. What, then, was I to do? I told him to stay for the present, and I would let him know by evening whether he could have the place permanently.

Accordingly I went at once to the provost-marshal's office, where I found an old friend, Lieutenant-Colonel Dick, in command, and told him the case. He said he could do nothing to interfere with the civil law in its regular process, but could secure me from violent intrusion, so that the man should have whatever advantages the mixed condition of civil and martial laws could rightly afford. That was

all I wanted, and he gave me the following
permit : —

The colored man named Archer Alexander, supposed
to be the slave of a rebel master, is hereby permitted to
remain in the service of W. G. Eliot until legal right to
his services shall be established by such party, if any, as
may claim them. Not to exceed thirty days unless extended.

F. A. DICK, *Lt. Col., Prov. Mar. Gen.*

FEB. 28, 1863.

Returning home, I told Archer that he could
stay at work until his master legally claimed
him, and one of the outhouses was made comfortable for his use. I doubt if there was a
happier man than he in St. Louis when he
heard the decision. He went right to work,
and by the end of two or three weeks the whole
family were attached to him. He was quiet,
gentle, diligent, and sufficiently intelligent.
The stable, garden, and the whole grounds soon
felt the difference. In fact, he was one of the
very best specimens of the negro race I had
ever known, and I began to think if I couldn't
in some way secure for him a legal right
to freedom. So I asked him more about himself, the name of his master, where he had lived,
and what made him run away. He told me,
among other things, that Judge Barton Bates

and family knew his people, and had often been at his master's house. I then went to Judge Bates, who said that Archer's master was a good Christian man, always kind to his "hands," and that he would most likely do what was just and right, though he "was not *particularly* what one would call a *loyal man.*" He promised to write to him at once, and give him my message ; viz., that Archer was at my place, and that I was willing to pay his full "market value" for sake of setting him free. I told the judge that I would go as high as six hundred dollars if necessary; but he answered that it would be twice too much, as things were.

The following is the letter he sent, a copy of which he gave to me a few days after : --

MR. ——.

SIR, — A gentleman of this city to-day stated to me that he would like to buy your man Archer, or Archie, if it could be done for a small sum, in order to emancipate him. He states that Archie is determined not to return to you, and that he believes he could not be compelled to return. If you choose to sell him, and will inform me of the amount that you will take for him, I will see that the gentleman is informed of it. I do not presume to advise or recommend any thing in the premises, and have no further agency in the matter.

Yours, etc.,

BARTON BATES·

The cautious wording of this letter shows the delicacy of the subject handled, at that time. No written answer came, but it served perhaps to give a hint to Archer's master where to find him.

After this I told Archer that I was trying hard to keep him, and, in fact, my mind was easy on the subject. I had no doubt that my offer would be accepted, as it would have been, under all the circumstances, by any reasonable man. But human passion is uncalculating of interest or right, and the verbal answer as reported to me, I hope incorrectly, was " that he didn't mean to play into the hands of any Yankee Abolitionist; that he'd have the nigger yet, and take it out of his black hide."

As time passed I became anxious, and told Archer to keep close about the house. The children were always following him when at work. He was very kind to them, and by the end of the month we were all as earnest to keep him as he was to stay. And so it came about, but not as I hoped and expected.

One lovely day, the last but one for which my provost-marshal protection was good, at about ten o'clock, I went out as usual to attend to my regular duties at " Washington University," and as I walked towards the Locust-street gate I stopped a moment to look at Archer with his plough, and the children at his heels. The plough he had found somewhere on the premises, had rigged it up in some fashion, so that my carryall-horse and harness could be put to service, and was busy to his heart's content. The two boys, Christy and Ed., seven and five years old, and the one-year-old baby, sister Rose, in the arms of Ellen her nurse, were the company. As they came towards me, and, reaching the limit of the garden lot, the horse was turned and the plough swung round with a scientific flourish, Archer bowed, and said, "Good-morning, sir," looking as happy as freedom could make him. Then they pushed on to make another furrow, the children shouting with pure enjoyment; and with the fruit-trees in full blossom, the birds singing in the branches, it was as pretty a rural picture as one can well imagine, close to a crowded and restless city. Looking just beyond and adjoining my grounds, I saw in the barrack-rooms of Uhrig's Cave the Union troops at the windows, within almost speaking distance, and the grand old flag flying over them. That gave me a feeling of satisfaction and safety.

As I lifted the gate-latch, a butcher-built man, whip in hand, accosted me, and asked if I hadn't a calf for sale, as he saw a cow in the pasture. He had a hang-dog, sneaking look, not in keeping with the day nor with my thoughts, and I answered him curtly that I had not, nor was I likely to have. At the same time I observed a close-covered wagon and two men standing by it, just across the street, with a rather suspicious appearance, and I paused for a minute; but as the butcher-looking man joined them and they seemed to be getting ready to move, and as I was in haste, I walked off with Hamilton's " Metaphysics " under my arm, and my mind intent upon the " law of the conditioned " and "excluded middle,"—how to explain it to a dozen not too eager youths, especially when I only half understood it myself.

At about one o'clock I returned, and found the whole family in terrified condition. The boys were crying, the nurse half distracted, and my wife calm, as she always is in troubled times, but with a suppressed excitement that startled me. They thought Archer was killed. As soon as I was well out of sight, the three men had come in, with clubs in hand, and, getting close to where Archer was working, said, " Is your name Archie?"—"Yes, sir, I've no 'casion to deny my name."—"Well, let go that horse, you runaway rascal, and come with us."—"No, sir, I'se here under pertection of the law."

He had no sooner said the word than one of them raised his bludgeon and knocked him down with a blow on the head. The others pulled out knives and pistols, and kicked him in the face. Then they handcuffed him and forcibly dragged the helpless man to their wagon, pushed him in, and drove off at the top of speed towards the city. The children and nurse ran to the house to tell the story. That was all I could learn. They had caught him, sure enough, and had probably got him far beyond my reach already. But, if so, it should not be for want of effort, on my part, to rescue him.

CHAPTER VI.

THE RESCUE.

FORTUNATELY the military protection was still in force, and, without taking off my hat or waiting for dinner, I started with quick step for the provost-marshal's office; no more abstractions in my mind, nor "law of the conditioned," but a plain duty to rescue the captive. Captain Dwight, who was on duty, heard my statement with great indignation. The nephew of Catherine Sedgwick was no friend of slavery. He looked at the "permit," questioned me closely, and then exclaimed, "I'll show these fellows what it is to defy this office!" Two detectives were summoned, one of them named John Eagan, to whom I shall always feel grateful; and Captain Dwight said, "I want you to listen to Dr. Eliot's statement." I repeated it carefully. "Now," said he, "have you got your pistols? Let me see them. Six-shooters? Well, are they loaded? All right. Now, one of you go down to the river and watch

every boat that leaves or is ready to leave. —
You, Eagan, go with this gentleman to his
house, find out all you can, follow up the hunt
until you take those scoundrels and release the
man, placing him again where he was taken
from."

"What shall we do, captain, if they refuse to
give him up?"

"Shoot them on the spot."

"We are to understand that, Captain Dwight,
shoot them on the spot?"

"Yes, shoot them dead if necessary.   Here
is your written authority to take the men."

"All right, sir," said Eagan: "we understand."

Eagan then walked out with me.   It seemed
ten miles instead of two to the gate where the
men had spoken to me in the morning.   While
I was describing them and their wagon, one of
my neighbors, Mr. Kelley, crossed the street
and said, "I can tell you something about that.
One of the men had a policeman's star on his
coat, and the wagon was a numbered city wagon.
The poor devil was mauled to death, and they
drove off quick.   I heard one of 'em say 'jail.'
I was afraid to interfere, and so were the soldiers, because of the star."

Eagan took down the wagon number, and, quietly turning to me, said, "Make yourself easy, sir. I'll have them before night. They can't get away. Where· shall I bring your man?"

"I shall be at the Western Sanitary Commission rooms, No. 11 5th Street, opposite the court-house, until ten o'clock this evening; after that, here."

"Oh, I'll have him long before that." And so we separated, my mind a little more at ease, but with only a half-hope at best.

At nine o'clock in the evening I was at the Sanitary Commission rooms, with Mr. Yeatman and other members, busy in opening several boxes of new garments just received from No. 13 Somerset Street, Boston.* We were in urgent need of them at the hospitals, and the rooms were in a blaze of light, so that we could work to advantage. Some one knocked loudly at the street door, and, looking up, I saw the two police-officers coming in with a colored man between them. It was Archer. He came forward, half blinded by the sudden glare of gaslight, and completely dazed, for he had not known where they were taking him.

* See Appendix II.

I came from behind the boxes, and, as he suddenly caught sight of me, he stopped, and, raising both his hands, exclaimed, "O Lord God! it's all right," and sank down on the floor helpless. "O Lord Jesus, it was you that done it!"

It seems, as I learned afterwards, that Eagan, having some clew in his search for Archer's captors, had traced them to the city jail, and then, posting his companion at a little distance outside, went into the outer office of the jail on Sixth Street, as if he had business there, and "in a promiscuous manner" began to talk to the jailer. The men whom he was looking for were right there, sitting at a table, drinking. They evidently had no fear of being followed, and perhaps thought they had the law on their side, for they were talking about their successful day's work. Eagan listened for a few minutes, and then, telling the jailer who he was, and that he had a military warrant to take those men, he stepped up to them and said, "Where is that nigger you are talking about?" — "Oh, he's in the jail there all right. He's off for Kentucky to-morrow. You never saw any thing slicker than the way we got him, right under the nose of that little abolition preacher. He was fooled completely." — "Well," said

Eagan, "that man was under military protection, and I want him. And, what's more, I've got a provost-marshal's warrant to take you : so come along."

They started to run, for, half tipsy as they were, they saw that they "had given themselves away." But just as they were getting out of the door, Eagan drew his pistol and exclaimed, "You are dead men if you take another step!" Just then the other police-officer came forward, and, seeing that they were trapped, they gave themselves up quietly. Eagan told the jailer to keep Archer safe until his return, and then took the captors down to the military prison, 5th and Myrtle Streets, where they were locked up for the night, not a little chop-fallen, and cursing their luck.

The officers then went back to the jail, and found Archer handcuffed, lying on the stone floor of a cell, dead asleep. They pushed him roughly, and as he raised his battered head, only half awake, they said, "Come, get up here, old man, you've got to go out of this." — "Lord, massa, what you goin' to do wid me ? I'se mose dead, anyhow." — "Never you mind, you've got to go, and that quick. Come, get up." He rose with difficulty. They took off

his handcuffs and led him out into the dark
without a word of explanation. It would seem
as if they meant to give him a sort of dramatic
surprise; at least, that was the effect. The
city jail was at that time only one block dis-
tant from the Commission rooms, and when in
less than five minutes, not knowing whether
he was in the hands of friends or enemies, he
came into the strong light of safety, it was to
him like passing from the blackness of despair
into the shelter of heaven.

"Why, Archer," I said to him, "you'd clean
given yourself up for lost, hadn't you?"—"No,
sir," he answered solemnly, with tears running down his bruised and swollen face. "No,
sir, I hadn't quite give up. I trusted in the
Lord. And *I sort a knowed you'd follow me up
and find me.*" By ten o'clock he was quietly
in his bed at his usual quarters, and I thanked
God with all my heart that the captors were
captured and their prisoner free.

The next day I obtained, by Captain Dwight's
advice, an unconditional protection for Archer,
which placed him in perfect safety, so far as he
could be in that uncertain time. I offered to
pay the police-officers for their efficient services, having obtained permission to do so;

but Eagan said, "No. They had done no more than their duty, and should be glad to do as much every day." * The captors of Archer were released as having acted ignorantly under the civil law, not knowing that he held a provost-marshal's permit.

In speaking of it the next day, Archer said to me, "I don't feel hard against them, sir, though they was rough and most killed me. But what hurt my feelins the most was to see that young man that showed them the way to me. I've toted him many a time about the field on my back when I was ploughin' and doin' my work on his father's place, whar was my home. I didn't think he could 'a' done it, sir. It wa'n't right in him, nohow. But the Lord forgive him for it. I'se free."

* I am glad to record the name of this faithful officer. His death occurred in the month of May, 1885, and I visited him at his home a few days previous to that event. He was a devout Catholic, an honest man, a good citizen. Some years ago, as his son informed me, he held in his custody a very wealthy man, a noted gambler, charged with aggravated crime. The prisoner offered him large sums of money, up to fifty thousand dollars, if he would connive at his escape and suppress the evidence. John Eagan refused to do it, preferring to remain comparatively poor, but thoroughly honest.

CHAPTER VII.

SAFETY.

BUT notwithstanding the full protection papers which I held, the state of social and political affairs was such that there could be no feeling of security to any runaway slave. Missouri was still a slave State, and the conflict between civil and martial law was at its height. I therefore made one more attempt to quiet the "legal claim to Archer's services" by getting a bill of sale from his master, and addressed the following letter to him :—

—— ——, *Esq.*

SIR,— About a week ago I sent a message to you by Judge Bates, that your man Archie was at my house, and asking you to set a price on him. Since that time he was forcibly taken from my place, but immediately brought back by order of the provost-marshal, under whose protection he has been since he first came to me, more than a month since. He has now papers which will protect him as long as martial law continues. But I prefer to obtain full legal title to his services if I can, and am still ready to buy him from you if you will fix a fair price, under the circumstances. I should emancipate him on the day of purchase. As to the price, I am willing to leave it to Governor Gamble and Judge Bates. My desire has been and is to do what is right in the premises. Yours, etc.,

W. G. ELIOT.

This note was sent through Governor Archibald Gamble, but no answer or notice of it ever came in return.

Our anxiety, therefore, continued, and we thought it best for Archer to be removed to a free State until the evidently coming freedom was fully established as the law of the land. As soon, therefore, as he was recovered from his hurts, I gave him a complete outfit of new clothes, which he had fairly earned, and took him by steamer to Alton, Ill. There he obtained a good place as farm-hand at the country home of one of my best friends, William H. Smith, whose hand and heart are and always have been open for every good work. Archer served him faithfully for six or seven months, at liberal wages, and when ready to return he had a hundred and twenty dollars to deposit in the Provident Savings Bank. But he had been anxious to get back to Missouri: for he looked to my place as home, and it was nearer to his wife and children. As soon, therefore, as things were sufficiently settled under the State gradual emancipation law, enacted June, 1863, he returned to Beaumont Place, theoretically, though not quite yet practically, on free soil. I still held myself ready to pay ransom-money to his master, to give perfect rest to the poor fellow's body and soul, but the opportunity was not offered. We had all by this time become so attached to him, and felt so great respect for his manly, patient character, that we would have spared neither cost nor pains to secure his freedom beyond all possible contingency. He settled down quietly to his work, earning his wages well, and taking care of every thing on the four-acre lot as if it were all his own. I never knew a man, white or black, more thoroughly Christian, according to the measure of light enjoyed, in all conduct and demeanor. He went regularly with me to the Church of the Messiah, of which I was pastor, and where I obtained for him the place of organ-blower. Every month he took his place with us at the Communion-table. But generally he kept close at home. He mixed very little with "his people," — that is, the colored people of the city, — and scarcely ever went out ,alone, because he was not yet quite over the fear of being again kid-napped. But he was contented, happy, and grateful.

CHAPTER VIII.

LOUISA.

FROM time to time Archer had word from his old home, through Germans who lived in the neighborhood, and early in November (1863) he managed to send messages to his wife Louisa. He wanted her to find out if they would sell her at a low price, and sent word that he had money to pay for her if they would. One day he brought a long letter from her for me to read to him. It had been dictated, and was in a lady's handwriting, as follows · —

NAYLOR'S STORE, Nov. 16, 1863.

MY DEAR HUSBAND, — I received your letter yesterday, and lost no time in asking Mr. Jim if he would sell me, and what he would take for me. He flew at me, and said I would never get free only at the point of the Baynot, and there was no use in my ever speaking to him any more about it. I don't see how I can ever get away except you get soldiers to take me from the house, as he is watching me night and day. If I can get away I will, but the people here are all afraid to take me away. He is always abusing Lincoln, and calls him an

78

old Rascoll. He is the greatest rebel under heaven. It is a sin to have him loose. He says if he had hold of Lincoln he would chop him up into mincemeat. I had good courage all along until now, but now I am almost heart-broken. Answer this letter as soon as possible.

I am your affectionate wife,

LOUISA ALEXANDER.

I asked him what he was going to do about it, and he said he'd just seen a German farmer that lived close by where Louisa was, who said he'd manage to get her away if she had anywhere to come to. "You see, sir, we've been married most thirty years, and we'se had ten chilluns, and we want to get togedder mighty bad." He said that three of the children, one of them a married woman, had already managed to get to St. Louis; and the youngest, Nellie, was with her mother, and would come too. His point was to know whether, if they *should* get off, they might come there to stay with him. "They wouldn't give no trouble, and there's plenty of room, and they could take keer of theirselves." I answered him that, if they were well treated, it would probably be best for them to stay where they were; in a few months freedom was almost sure, and then they could come and go as they pleased; but if they came I should not drive them away, though they'd have to take their chances. He said he knew that, but the German had told him "Louisa was having the roughest kind of a time, and, now that they suspicioned her, her life wasn't safe if they got mad at her." There it rested for a week or two, when it was reported one Sunday morning at breakfast-table, that Louisa and Nellie had arrived just before daylight.

The German farmer had kept his word. He had told Louisa that on Saturday even-ing, soon after sunset, he should be driving his wagon along the lane near her cabin, and that if they could manage to get down there, he would pick them up, and put them on the road. So at dusk they strolled down that way separately, without bonnets or shawls, so as not to attract notice. Nellie was thirteen years old, a smart girl, and well understood the plan. Meeting at a place agreed upon, they only had to wait two or three minutes before their deliverer came. He was driving an ox-team, his wagon being loaded with corn shucks and stalks loosely piled. Under these, arranged for the purpose, he made them crawl, and covered them up with skilful carelessness, so that they had breathing-place, but were completely concealed. He then drove on very leisurely, walking by the oxen, with good moonlight to show the way. When they had gone about a mile, one of their master's family, on horseback, overtook them, and asked the farmer if he had seen "two niggers, a woman and a gal," anywhere on the road. He stopped his team a minute, so as "to talk polite," and said, "Yes, I saw them at the crossing, as I came along, standing, and looking scared-like, as if they were waiting for somebody; *but I have not seen them since.*" Literal truth is sometimes the most ingenious falsehood.

The man looked up and down the road, turned quickly, and went back to see if he could find the trace in another direction.

The farmer, chuckling to himself, drove on as fast as his oxen could travel, and before daylight was at the place where he had promised to bring his human freight. Archer paid him twenty dollars for his night's work.

After all, it was but small loss to the master, for on the eleventh day of January, 1865, the immediate and total Emancipation Law was passed by the State Convention at St. Louis, and Missouri was a free State. I was present at that grand consummation, and remember it with unspeakable gratitude. (See *Am. Cyclop.*, art. "Missouri.")

But Louisa's coming brought peace of mind to Archer, who seemed to hold his wife and children in as tender regard as if he had been free from the beginning. Two others of his daughters soon found him out. He also learned of the death on the battle-field of his son Tom (named for his young master, Thomas Delaney), who had enlisted in the Union army, among the first colored recruits, and was killed in a brave charge by negro troops at Tilton Head. I subsequently obtained full record of his enlistment and services and death, and, on application to the proper authorities, his back pay and bounty-money were paid to Archer. Very proud was he that his son had served and died in the cause of freedom. " I couldn't do it myself," he said, " but I thank the Lord my boy did it."

CHAPTER IX.

FREEDOM AND REST.

FOR two years after the war of secession had ended, Archer remained in my service; he then set up housekeeping for himself. His wife, Louisa, had died nearly a year before, under somewhat peculiar circumstances. She became anxious to visit her old home " to get her things ; " that is, her bed and clothes, and little matters of furniture, that " Mr. Jim " sent word she could get *if she would come for them.* We advised her not to go, as they were not worth much, and there might be some risk involved ; but she "honed" for them, and went. Two days after getting there, she was suddenly taken sick and died. The particulars could not be learned, but " the things " were sent down by the family. Archer mourned for her not quite a year, and then married a young woman named Judy, twenty-five years old, with whom he moved to his own hired house, feeling, no doubt, that it was one more step of freedom.

Their housekeeping was on a very small scale. A good part of his earnings came from my family; and there were times of close poverty, though never of distress. A long life of slavery had unfitted him for the sharp competitions of freedom in a city life, and in many things he was only a grown-up child. As a mere matter of physical comfort, his slavery days were better, his work less wearing, his daily bread more easily earned, his sickness better cared for. But he felt the manliness of freedom, and was happy in it. He used it, too, without abusing it, was strictly temperate, kept out of debt, and was always ready to help others, even beyond the limit of prudence. Shiftless and worthless negroes imposed upon him, and not a few claimed kindred to himself or wife. But he had in his humble sphere a dignified and happy life, and was never unfaithful to his Christian faith and principles.

At the funeral of his second wife, Judy, whose death occurred only a year before his own, when I was conducting the services, I observed, in the lap of one of the colored women attending, a child about three years old, perfectly white and very pretty, and inquired afterwards whose it was.

It appeared that three months before, the little one had been left entirely destitute by her mother, who had, on her death-bed, given her up by a written paper to Archer and Judy. She was therefore, after a manner, their legally adopted child, and Archer was sadly at loss how to provide for her. I assumed care of her, and Archer had the satisfaction, some months before his death, of seeing her well provided for in a home where she would be educated and trained for a useful life. I also learned concerning her that on her mother's side she could claim descent from a very respectable Scotch family; but unfortunately the number of marriage ceremonies had not kept quite equal pace with the genealogical steps, and the waif was unacknowledged.

Six months afterwards, when she was under care of a lady who treated her with a mother's tenderness, Archer asked permission to visit her. He went with his negro heart full of love and pride, expecting a loving welcome. But it happened that in all those months the little one, who was only four years old, had seen no colored persons, and she had quite forgotten her kind benefactor. So when he came into the room with a broad smile, saying to her, "Oh, here she is! Come to your old daddy!" she did not know him, but, half scared, made up a lip, and ran for shelter to her lady protector. Then she turned and looked at him with big eyes, with no shadow of recollection. He paused, tears ran down his cheeks, and he soon left quite heavy-hearted. "It cut into me," he said when I next saw him: "it cut sharp into me like a knife. My feelins was hurt drefful bad. She'd clean done forgot me, and was skeered at me. Many a time I had hugged her in my bosom. But I ain't of much account, nohow."

It was a real grief to him, poor fellow, and I cannot think of it now without pain. He ended by saying, "I thank the Lord she's got good friends, and will grow up to be a lady." It is a small incident, too trifling perhaps for mention; but to that humble, loving heart it was a real and abiding grief.

The remainder of Archer's troubled life was marked by sadness and suffering, without possibility of relief. The infirmities of age were upon him, and an internal rupture prevented him from any work except what a child might have done. At a time when I was absent from the city with my family, he had a severe attack,

and it became absolutely necessary for him to
be taken to the city hospital for the best sur-
gical treatment. At this the simple-hearted
fellow was sorely mortified. His pride was as
much hurt as if he had been sent to the alms-
house as a pauper. But he found himself so
kindly and generously treated by Dr. Dean
and assistants, that he soon became recon-
ciled, and understood that all was done for the
best.

On my return he was removed, comparatively
restored, to comfortable rooms near my residence, where he was well nursed and cared
for. I believe that he wanted for nothing that
kindness could supply. But the end soon came.
He gave me verbal directions for disposal
among his kindred of his little property, a few
articles of furniture of small value, and his last
words were a prayer of thanksgiving that he
died in freedom.

His funeral, at which I officiated, took place
from the African Methodist Church, on Lucas
Avenue, and was largely attended. He was
decently buried in the Centenary Burial-Ground,
near Clayton Court-House, followed to his last
resting-place by many friends. A part of the
expenses of his long sickness, and all the

funeral charges, were defrayed from the funds of the Western Sanitary Commission.*

It is the record of a humble life, but one which was conformed, up to the full measure of ability, to the law of the gospel. I have felt as proud of the long-continued friendship and confidence of Archer Alexander as of any one I have known.

He was, I believe, the last fugitive slave taken in Missouri under the old laws of slavery. His freedom came directly from the hand of President Lincoln, by provost-marshal authority, and his own hands had helped to break the chains that bound him. His oldest son had given his life to the cause.

When I showed to him the photographic picture of the " Freedom's Memorial " monument, soon after its inauguration in Washington, and explained to him its meaning, and that he would thus be remembered in connection with Abraham Lincoln, the emancipator of his race, he laughed all over. He presently sobered down and exclaimed, "Now I'se a white man! Now I'se free! I thank the

* See Appendix III.

good Lord that he has 'livered me from all my troubles, and I'se lived to see this."

> " No sea
> Swells like the bosom of a man set free !
> A wilderness is rich with liberty."

A monumental stone will soon be placed to mark the spot where he was captured as a fugitive slave, with this inscription : —

ARCHER ALEXANDER.
FROM SLAVERY TO FREEDOM, March 30, 1863.

CHAPTER X.

SLAVERY IN THE BORDER STATES.

I HAVE spoken of slavery in Missouri as existing in its mildest form, and under many alleviations, by force of prevailing public opinion.

In saying this, however, I do not mean that no cruelties, and no acts of gross injustice, were committed under the slavery system as I have seen it in St. Louis, nor that the public mind was so elevated as to condemn all such wrongs by open censure. That would be untrue, and I speak only comparatively in my reference to the subject. It would be pleasant to forget all that is painful in the past, and to say of the institution of slavery and all connected with it, let the dead past bury its dead. But such forgetting would be unwise, and would have the effect of debarring the rising generation from many of the most important lessons that the past teaches. It would also prevent us from forming a just estimate, both of the evils from which as a people we have been delivered, and of the national blessings we now enjoy.   The prophet Isaiah, when calling the attention of his people to the glory of the present and future, says, "Look to the hole of the pit whence ye were digged;" and equally may we say, when men are complaining of political and social wrongs, and of the evils that so greatly abound, Remember what your fathers bore; remember the fearful wrongs, formerly so common, defended by law, sustained by public opinion, regarded as incurable, which have now become impossible, the record of which is now almost beyond belief.

Notwithstanding the comparative humanity of slavery as an institution in Missouri, I can truthfully say that there is nothing in all the scenes of "Uncle Tom's Cabin" as given by Mrs. Stowe, to which I cannot find a parallel in what I have myself seen and known in St. Louis itself, previously to the war of secession. Let me enter here on record a few of the details.

On my coming to St. Louis, 27th of November, 1834, one of the first things I heard was of

a colored girl who had been whipped so severely
by a "gentleman" who lived not far from.
where I lodged, that she died before night.
The gentleman was in the very best circles as
to wealth and surroundings, an officer in the
United States army, high in rank, distinguished
in appearance, and of Herculean strength.
The girl was suspected of having stolen a key
with intention of rifling the bureau-drawers of
her mistress, and was whipped to compel her
to confess. The gentleman was indicted and
thrown into jail, where he was visited by a
fellow-officer of the United States army (his
subordinate), who afterwards became my intimate friend, and told me the particulars. By
change of venue the case was carried into St.
Charles County, and a verdict of *not guilty* was
rendered, although of the facts there could be no
dispute. The "public" were shocked, but the
feeling was of no endurance. The gentleman's
standing was not permanently, if at all, affected.
No notice of the transaction was taken by the
military authorities. It did not impede his
advance to still higher grades of military service in after years.

Forty-five years afterward, when thinking of
the events as narrated, I could hardly trust my

memory, so atrocious did they seem, and I
wrote to the friend above referred to for con-
firmation.   He replied as follows : —

JUNE 17, 1880.

MY DEAR SIR, — Major —— did whip a negro woman
so brutally that she died from the effects of the whipping.   My recollection of the matter is that she did not
die under the lash, but was so lacerated and beaten that
she was barely alive, and died within a day or two after
the whipping : . . . was indicted by the grand jury for
murder or manslaughter, I do not remember which.
He was put in the jail in St. Louis to await his trial, and
I visited him in jail.   I am strongly of the impression
that the indictment was for murder, and that bail was
refused ; and the fact that he was put in jail is confirma-
tory of that impression.   Whether this was in 1834 or
before that, I do not remember.   He did not dare to
come to trial in St. Louis, and got a change of venue to
St. Charles County.   The woman was the slave of his
wife or his wife's sister, and was accused of having
stolen a key, which she denied, and he whipped her to
make her confess it.   Several years afterwards, in con-
versing with a lady, now Mrs. Major ——, about " Uncle
Tom's Cabin," I said, " You and I know parallel cases to
every one in that book."   She said, " Yes, except the
case of Legree." — "Ah, madam," I said, "you forget "
. . . and she assented.

N. J. E.

In the following year, a free mulatto man,
who had committed some petty offence, and

was known to be a troublesome fellow, was in charge of two police-officers on the way to jail, which was then on Sixth and Chestnut Streets, when he suddenly drew a knife, stabbed one of his captors fatally, and the other dangerously. He attempted escape; but it was on the open street, by the court-house, and the cry for help brought a crowd who caught and carried him to jail. One of his victims died on the spot. The other, known as a faithful officer, was thought to be dying. Intense excitement prevailed; and a mob, headed by many good citizens, went to the jail, forcibly took the negro out, carried him to a tree which stood where the Public School Polytechnic building now stands, and were proceeding to hang him. Some one cried out, "BURN HIM!" The word was immediately taken up by the crowd. The man was tied to the trunk of the tree; fence-rails and dry wood in abundance were brought and piled up around him. Several leading and prominent men, whom everybody knew, were active in bringing the rails with their own hands. There was no secrecy or disguise attempted. The deed was accomplished, the man was burned to death, and his body (or the remnant of it) was left there until the next day. Fortunately for me, I knew nothing of all this until the morning, after breakfast, when I was sent for by the family of the wounded officer.

The show of judicial investigation was gone through; but, although the names of a dozen of the actors were known to everybody, it was passed over as the act of an irresponsible mob, and was freely spoken of by many as a good warning to free negroes.

It was the same year when William Lloyd Garrison, whose name is now the pride of Massachusetts, was hounded almost to death, and dragged through the streets of Boston with a rope round his body, good citizens looking on, because of his too bold attacks on the patriarchial institution of the Southern States. The roots of slavery had struck very deep, and its branches were wide-spread, casting dark shadows over the whole land. Thank God, it was cut down, and its roots have withered away!

Several years later, in 1839–40, I was living on Market Street, near Third, just back of the National Hotel. My "study" was over the dining-room in the back building, the windows looking out upon the yard of a neighbor, whose house fronted on Third Street. One day I was startled by a terrible scream, and, going to the window, saw under an open shed a young mulatto woman tied up to the joist by her thumbs, so that her feet scarcely touched the ground, stripped from her shoulders to the hips, and a man standing by her with cowhide-whip in hand. He had paused for a moment from his scourging to see if she would "give in." I opened the window and called out to him. He told me "to shut up and mind my own business." But he feared publicity just enough to untie the victim and stop his brutality for the time. I shut up my book and went straight before the grand jury, which was then in session, and entered complaint against the man, who was a person of fair respectability. A true bill was found, and he was brought before the criminal court for trial. The court was at the time held in the basement room of the Unitarian Church, where I was pastor, having been let for the purpose while the court-house was undergoing repair. (Those were primitive days in St. Louis.) I was called as witness, and the case was fully proved. The offence of the colored girl was her un-

willingness to "submit to the wishes" of her
master. The judge charged accordingly, and
there was no room for acquittal. Neverthe-
less the verdict was "not guilty," because, as
afterwards declared, the penalty fixed by law
was thought to be too severe. It had been
strongly so represented by the counsel for
defendant. Attempt was also made to invalidate my testimony as that of a sentimental
young preacher who knew nothing about slavery. That was a strong point to make.

Not many years before the outbreak of the
war, when public opinion had very much
advanced, an old colored man came to see me
to ask if I could not do something to get his
daughter Melinda out of the slave-jail, and
prevent her from being "sold South." Her
master and mistress were persons of high
respectability, members of an Orthodox Church,
and until lately she had always been treated
kindly, as an indulged servant who had grown
up with the children of the household. As a
child she had been their playmate, almost on
equal terms, as was not an uncommon case in
Southern-educated families. But as the girls
grew into young ladies, the slave-girl had not

been sensible enough to see the growing dis-
tinction between herself and them, and had
become "sassy." She had been several times
very impudent to her mistress, who became
angry with her, and insisted upon her being
sold; and not only so, but that she should be
sent out of the city. Her husband assented,
and had placed her in one of the slave-jails,
at corner of Sixth and Locust Streets, to go
with the next "gang" Southward, where her
"attractive appearance would command a
high price."

The old man said all he wanted was *time;*
that he had bought his own freedom, and had
just finished paying for himself; that the
house where he was porter would help him
to pay for Melinda, if Mr. —— would only let
him have her and "pay up gradual," but that
Mr. —— had said she'd got to be sold out of
the city. I told him that I didn't know what
to do about it, but that, although I was not
acquainted with Mr. ——, I would go and see
if there was any chance. This I did, and
found the gentleman in his counting-room on
Main Street, a wholesale store of leading
importance. He received me very politely;
and when I had explained my purpose, telling

him the condition of things, I asked him if he would not sell the girl on my guaranty, so that her father could have her, either in his own name or that of some friend. He said no; that he had promised his wife to sell her *away from the city*, where she would give her girls no trouble; and that she was not for sale here. "Well," I said, "if that is your fixed determination, I can't help it, for under the law you have a right to do as you please. But one thing I can do :· I can make the facts known. I therefore now offer you the price, whatever it is, that you expect for the girl, so that she may stay with her father." — "All right," he answered as I rose to leave, "if you will come in to-morrow morning, I'll let you know." In the morning he agreed to the proposal ; stipulating, however, that the bill of sale should be made out *to me*, eight hundred dollars as the price, one-third cash, and balance with eight per cent interest, and my indorsement to the notes. It was arranged in an hour's time, and for two hours thereafter I was Melinda's legal owner. I went directly to the jail, showed to the slave-dealer my bill of sale and an order for delivery of the chattel, and went in to see her. She was waiting, forlorn and cheerless, a good-looking girl of eighteen years, knowing nothing of the transfer. Glad enough was she to go to her father, who received her thankfully. *She was then already a free woman.* He raised the cash payment at once, and I never heard a syllable of the notes, which must have been duly provided for by him.

The transaction, however, as it was near being completed, was in substance not an uncommon one. "Likely young mulatto gals" were apt to be impudent, and impudence or unmanageableness was punishable as a crime. St. Louis was fast becoming a slave-market, and the supply was increasing with the demand. Often have I seen "gangs" of negroes handcuffed together, two and two, going through the open street like dumb driven cattle, on the way to the steamboat for the South. Large fortunes were made by the trade; and some of those who made them, under thin cover of agency, were held as fit associates for the best men on 'change.

These illustrations of slavery as it was, and as I have seen it, are given in their simplest outline. Let them be dramatized, — not exaggerated, but brought out in the colors of real life, with suffering and helpless human beings as the victims of legalized brutality, ungoverned passion, and unbridled lust, — and there is nothing worse to be found, in the " Fool's Errand," by Tourgee, or in the historical pictures of Harriet Beecher Stowe.

One other instance of the same character, the truth of which I know, although not personally interested in its details, is given here.

In the year 185-, Mr. M., a well-known citizen of St. Louis and a man of family, held as slave a mulatto woman, personable and well-mannered, with whom his relations were intimate, and two children were born to them. He then gave to her " free papers," renouncing all claim to her services. She left the city soon after; and being arrested in Peoria, Ill., on suspicion as a fugitive slave, he sent a written statement of her freedom, on strength of which she was released. Subsequently he induced her to return to St. Louis, and then proposed to renew his former relations with her. She refused, pleading that she was a church-member, a reformed woman, and wished to keep free from her former sins. He then asked her to bring her manumission papers to him, that he might correct some informalities in them, so as to save further trouble.. She did so, and he put them in the fire. It seemed that they were informal, had never been entered on record, and had no legal validity. Judge Gamble, to whom the matter was referred by some humane persons who knew the facts, gave his opinion that there was no legal remedy, although it was an outrageous wrong. "The claim was legally perfect, and the power of the master was absolute."

He took her, accordingly, by the sheriff, and placed her and her children in Lynch's slave-jail, with orders to send them South for sale. They were, however, temporarily released, and held under security bond for their return, for several months, when, after the best legal counsel had exhausted every means of rescue or reprieve, the law compelled their being again placed in the jail, subject to their owner's will. His legal wife, who knew all the facts, refused to hear of any thing in their favor, and urged their immediate sale to "a Southern plantation, where they should be well worked." But fortunately her own son, the half-brother of the negro woman's children, either through compassion or shame, insisted upon their being sold to a gentleman who had been active in their behalf, and by whom this narrative is given to me. He sent them, legally manumitted, to a free State; and so, as by special providence, they were snatched from a fate worse than death. No thanks to the laws of slavery. I believe no members of Mr. M.'s family now live in Missouri.

As an illustration of the almost impossibility of securing the slave from the worst hardships of the system, I give the following extract from the letter of a personal friend, a man of great intelligence, and, so far as my acquaintance goes, of unequalled humanity.

St. Louis, Feb. 16, 1885.

. . . I have read your manuscript carefully, and can testify of my own knowledge that it is a perfectly true and fair delineation of slavery as it existed from the forties down. I could easily confirm all you have said, and much more. My experience commenced in Tennessee, on a farm, before I attained my majority, as the owner of some twenty-five or thirty negroes, men, women, and children, all of whom were purchased, with one or two exceptions, in families, from one man. For each family I built a separate house, and taught all who were willing, to read, although the same was forbidden by law. Four years later it became necessary for me to remove, to take charge of a city business-house. I sold my farm, and disposed of all my negroes, to a gentleman who had been a lifelong friend of my family, taking for them a mere nominal sum, in order to secure them a good master, who would keep them all together. My friend placed the negroes on a plantation that he had purchased in the neighborhood. He put it in charge of a kinsman from a free State, in whom he had confidence, and who was to receive, as compensation for his services, one-fourth of the net earnings. But the overseer proved to be a hard task-master; and four or five years later, in visiting my old home, I called to see the purchaser of my old servants, to ask about them. He had a sad tale to tell. Many of the negroes had died from overwork and bad treatment from "the Yankee overseer." The place was brought in debt, and the rest of them were sold under the hammer, singly, for the best price they would bring, and scattered far and wide. So all my efforts, and the pecuniary sacrifice which I made to keep them together, were of no avail,

It was this experience that first taught me the inherent evils of slavery, although I had always been a gradual emancipationist. The perpetration of other wrongs that I witnessed as I advanced in life so impressed me that I gave freedom to all the domestics whom I owned, which was some years before the presidential election of 1856.

I hope to see your manuscript in print. Many persons of this day have no conception of what slavery was, and how it was regarded by very many very good people. Your description is just and appreciative.

J. E. Y.

Nearly all of those to whom reference has been made, either directly or indirectly, in this chapter, have passed away, and personal interest in the special facts given has well nigh ceased.   But everywhere in the former slave States the memory of like cases of hardship and suffering remains.   In every precinct, city, village, or town, with whatever diversity of details, the same general record might be made.

Therefore it is that in the Southern even more than in the Northern States, the prayer of thanksgiving continually ascends that by the over-ruling providence of God the days of Slavery have ended.   In the previous pages I have said that no freedman would consent to return to the best conceivable condition of bondage ; equally true is it that no former slave-holder, of any intelligence, can be found who would consent again to become a " master." And this, not chiefly because of the growing conviction that free labor is most profitable, but far more because of the moral and social deliverance which freedom has conferred.   If it were within the range of possibility to re-establish the institution of slavery as it was thirty years ago, and if such change were proposed, the resistance of the Southern States would be the most-emphatic. It is true that "they have been led by a way they had not known" to this great deliverance, but they now understand that, in every sense, it has become a supreme benediction.

There are many conflicting interests, both political and financial, to be settled between the North and South, for which there will be abundant need of patience and mutual forbearance. But the one great cause of contention has been forever removed, and before the present generation has passed, the North and South, East and West, will be the most closely united people on the face of the earth.

CHAPTER XI.

ELIJAH P. LOVEJOY.

IN Missouri the social struggle between freedom and slavery began with the persecution
and martyrdom of Elijah Parish Lovejoy, between the years 1833 and 1837. It was a
tragic beginning, but less than thirty years
later it ended with the triumphant emancipation decree of a convention of the State, Jan.
11, 1865, adopted by almost unanimous vote
(only two votes in the negative), as follows :—

" *Be it ordained by the people of the State of Missouri, in
convention assembled,* That hereafter in this State there
shall be neither slavery nor involuntary servitude, except in punishment of crime, whereof the party shall
have been duly convicted ; and all persons held to service or labor as slaves are hereby declared free."

It is worthy of note that Missouri was the
only slave State in the Union, which, of its own
accord, thus gave freedom to its slaves. President Lincoln's proclamation of freedom was a
war measure, taking effect only in the seceded
States, and even there of doubtful legal valid-

ity, until a constitutional amendment had been adopted by a two-thirds vote of the whole Union. Then Kentucky and Maryland became free States. But Missouri had already been established as a free State by her own acts, — first by a gradual emancipation ordinance, June, 1863; and finally by the conclusive act of January, 1865.

The contrast is all the greater when we look back to the days of Elijah P. Lovejoy; and a few pages of that record may here not be out of place. I am indebted for nearly all the details to several recent articles in the "Globe Democrat" of St. Louis, and in the "St. Louis Republican," the latter of which are from the pen of Mr. Thomas Dimmock, one of the ablest editors of that well-known and influential journal.

Mr. Lovejoy first came to St. Louis in 1827, being at the time twenty-five years of age. "Having a decided taste and talent for journalism, he naturally drifted into it, and in 1828 became editor of the long since forgotten 'Times,' then advocating the claims of Henry Clay. His editorial work made him quite popular with the Whig party, and might have opened the way to political advancement; but in the winter of 1831–32, during a religious revival, his views of life underwent a radical change, and he united with the Second Presbyterian Church, then in charge of Rev. W. S. Potts. Believing he had a call to the sacred office, he entered the Princeton Theological School in the spring of 1832, where he remained until April, 1833, when he received his ministerial credentials. In the autumn of the same year he returned to St. Louis, then a city of seven thousand inhabitants, and, yielding to the solicitations of many friends, established a weekly religious newspaper, called the 'Observer,' the friends furnishing the necessary funds, and the entire management being intrusted to him. The first number appeared Nov. 29, 1833. In the spring of 1834 he publicly announced his anti-slavery principles, and thus began the bitter warfare, which finally cost him his life. He was not, however, what was then popularly known as an abolitionist. He favored gradual emancipation, with the consent, compensation, and assistance of the slave-owners; and this should be considered in our estimate of the character and conduct of the man, and of those who hounded him to death."

In October, 1835, an earnest and affectionate letter was addressed to Mr. Lovejoy, signed
by nine of his principal supporters, all of whom
were men of commanding influence in St.
Louis. Among them were Archibald Gamble,
W. S. Potts, Hamilton R. Gamble, and Beverly
Allen. They represented in every sense the
best citizens of the city and State. They
pleaded with him as Christians and patriots,
ending with this appeal : " We do not claim to
prescribe your course as an editor, but we hope
that the concurring opinions of so many persons having the interests of your paper and of
religion both at heart may induce you to dis-
trust your own judgment, and so far change
the character of the ' Observer ' as to pass over
in silence every thing connected with the subject of slavery."

What his reply was may be understood,
says the " Globe Democrat," Nov. 16, 1884,
from the following memorandum on the back
of the original letter, made only two weeks before his death : —

I did not yield to the wishes here expressed, and in
consequence have been persecuted ever since. But I
have kept a good conscience in the matter, and that re-
pays me for all I have suffered, or can suffer. I have

sworn eternal opposition to slavery, and, by the blessing
of God, I will never go back.   E. P. L.

Oct. 24, 1837.

In July, 1836, the patience of St. Louis was
exhausted, and Mr. Lovejoy having announced
his intention of removing to Alton, Ill., a mob
of citizens entered his office, and destroyed
the furniture, and scattered the types, by way
of a parting expression of hatred and con-
tempt.   As I remember it, very few persons,
even among the best citizens, expressed either
regret or condemnation.

He fared no better in Alton.   His first press
was destroyed as soon as landed, and a second
one met the same fate in the following August.
The whole population was stirred up against
him, as would have been the case at that day
in any town of the United States.   Meeting
after meeting was held, at which his proceed-
ings were denounced.   At one of these meet-
ings, standing quite alone, he said, —

"But, gentlemen, as long as I am an American citizen,
and as long as American blood runs in these veins, I
shall hold myself at liberty to speak, to write, and to
publish, whatever I please on any subject, being
amenable to the laws of my country for the same."

"For these immortal principles," says Mr.

Dimmock, "Lovejoy laid down his life. His perfect honesty and honor were never doubted, nor was his superb moral and physical courage. He was a rare combination of bravery and tenderness; as brave as a lion, as tender as a woman." In what may be justly regarded as his dying appeal, five days before his violent death, in presence of a crowd of incensed enemies, he spoke as follows:—

"MR. CHAIRMAN,—I plant myself down on my unquestionable *rights*, and the question to be decided is, whether I am to be protected in the exercise and enjoyment of those rights,—*that is the question, sir,*—whether my property shall be protected; whether I shall be suffered to go home to my family at night without being assailed and threatened with tar and feathers, and assassination; whether my afflicted wife, whose life has been in jeopardy from continued alarm and excitement, shall, night after night, be driven from a sickbed into the garret to escape the brickbats and violence of the mobs,—*that, sir, is the question.* [Here the speaker burst into tears.] Forgive me, sir, that I have thus betrayed my weakness. It was allusion to my family that overcame my feelings; not, sir, I assure you, from any fears on my part. I have no personal fears. Not that I feel able to contest the matter with the whole community: I know perfectly well I am not. I know, sir, you can tar and feather me, hang me, or put me in the Mississippi, without the least difficulty. But what then? Where shall I go? I have been made to feel that if I am not safe in Alton I shall not be safe anywhere. I recently visited St. Charles to bring home my family. I was torn from their frantic embrace by a mob. I have been beset day and night in Alton. And now, if I leave here and go elsewhere, violence may overtake me in my retreat, and I have no more claim upon the protection of any other community than I have upon this; and I have concluded, after consultation with my friends and earnestly seeking counsel of God, to remain at Alton, and here insist on protection in the exercise of my rights. If the civil authorities refuse to protect me, I must look to God; and if I die, I am determined to make my grave in Alton."

Five days later, Nov. 7, 1837, a citizen mob took him at his word, beset him at his printing-office, and murdered him. His body was privately interred, pains being taken to conceal the place of burial, from fear that the mob violence would desecrate his grave. But after the lapse of many years, Mr. Dimmock succeeded in finding the spot, and having purchased the ground, he has presented it, in trust for the colored people of Alton, to Mr. Isaac H. Kelley. It will be hereafter properly cared for; and at an early day a suitable monument will be erected, in memory of the proto-martyr of freedom, in the United States, who at the early age of thirty-five years gave his life in vindication of the great cause to which he had consecrated it.

I place the record here, partly as illustrative of the times when the events occurred, but still more because I think that it helps to explain the rapid growth, in St. Louis and Missouri, of public opinion on the subjects of domestic slavery and freedom of speech. The blood of the martyr is the seed not only of the Church, but of truth and liberty. Hundreds of those who half approved of the outrages as they took place, were led by sober second thought not only to condemn them, but to hate the cause for which they had been committed.

In the great national exodus from slavery to freedom, Elijah P. Lovejoy was a pioneer, and his memory should be held in special honor to the last day of our national existence.

Appendix I.

RELIGIOUS MARRIAGE OF SLAVES.

THE time will come when this statement will seem almost incredible. The usage, considered as a barbarism for which no religious defence would be possible, is bad enough. But to give it the sanction of religion, the religion of Jesus Christ, and to invoke the Divine blessing upon a marriage which was no marriage at all, but simply a concubinage which the master's word might at any moment invalidate, seems at first beyond all manner of excuse. Yet it was done, and that not only by individual ministers of Christ, but by authority of ecclesiastical conventions. The resolutions to that effect went upon record in Methodist, Baptist, Presbyterian churches, declaring that the separation of husband and wife under the laws of slavery, by the removal of either party, was to be regarded as "civil death," sundering the bonds, and leaving both parties free to make another marriage contract. Slavery, by necessity of the case, abolished all family ties, — of husband and wife, of parents and children, of brothers and sisters, — except so far as the convenience of the master might be suited by their recognition. Legal sanction there was none. But the sham-service which the law scorned to recognize was rendered by the ministers of the gospel of Christ. I have witnessed it, but could never bring myself to take part in such pretence.

And yet I feel compelled by truth to say that, among all the alleviations of slavery, there was none greater than this. While the nominal relation continued at all, it was made sacred to the slave husband and wife, and the affectionate African nature was comforted and sustained by it. It was a strong motive to good behavior, it promoted decency in social intercourse, it tended towards keeping the slave-family together, and was some restraint upon masters — a great restraint upon the better class of them — against arbitrary separation by sale: in short, it was one of the fearful anomalies of a brutal and barbarous social system existing among a civilized, Christian people.

The question was fully discussed by the Savannah River Baptist Association of Ministers in 1835; and the decision was, " that such separation, among persons situated as slaves are, is civilly a separation by death, and that in the sight of God it would be so viewed. To forbid second marriages in such case would be to expose the parties to church censure for disobedience to their masters, and to the spirit of that command which regulates marriage among Christians. The slaves are not free agents, and a dissolution by death is not more entirely without their consent and beyond their control than by such separation."

Truly the logic of slavery was the destruction of humanity.

APPENDIX II.

Soon after the battle at Wilson's Creek, Missouri, in which the Union troops under General Lyon sustained a seeming defeat but gained a real victory, the sufferings of our soldiers in the field and hospitals were very great, and an appeal for relief was published in the St. Louis papers by the Western Sanitary Commission. Attention was called to this in the Boston "Transcript" by my sister, Mrs. Hannah Dawes Lamb, who volunteered to receive at her home, No. 13 Somerset Street, all funds and new clothing or goods, to be forwarded by Adams's Express to St. Louis, free of charge. A most liberal response was made, not only in Boston, but from every part of New England. Every week large boxes were packed, and remittances of money daily came in, without special agencies or solicitation. In course of the war the full value, in money or new goods, of $40,000, came to us through that channel. Many thousands of the sick and wounded, including prisoners, who were treated exactly as our own men, had reason to thank God for the kindly patriotism of New England women. Every Boston box made our eyes glad, for every article sent was the best of its kind.

Appendix III.

The Western Sanitary Commission, originally established by order of Major-General Frémont, and afterwards recognized and made permanent by the secretary of war, Edwin M. Stanton, is still in active working existence. All of its members — James E. Yeatman, J. B. Johnson, George Partridge, Carlos S. Greeley, and W. G. Eliot — are yet living. It has a residuum of its funds, amounting to over $50,000, well invested, by use of which children and families of "Union soldiers," and at times other persons, are reminded of the kindly charities that grew out of the fearful fratricidal war.

The total amount in cash and sanitary stores received by the Commission during the war, was officially reported at $4,270,998.55, the whole of which was used for the humane and sanitary purposes for which it was given, the total costs of distribution having been less than one per cent. The surplus above named was a part of the interest earnings which accrued from the excellent management of the treasurer, Carlos S. Greeley.

Besides the hospital work for the sick and wounded, the Western Sanitary Commission was intrusted by the authorities with the care and relief of Union refugees, and of fugitive slaves from the South. Many thousands of both these classes of sufferers thronged to St. Louis, generally in wretched condition, not only impoverished, but thriftless and inefficient. In one way or another they were taken care of until some sort of

APPENDIX III.

work was found by which they could earn the...
Special funds were liberally contributed, chiefly...
New England, for such uses.

Throughout the war, quite up to its close in 1865, many of the orders issued by the president of the Commission were signed, " By order of Major-General J. C. Frémont," being regarded by his successors as outside of army regulations, and beyond the authority usually exercised by generals in command. In fact, when I first submitted the form of organization to Dr. De Camp, United States medical director, Sept. 5, 1861, he promptly said that it was unusual and irregular, but that it would be of great service if authorized by the commanding general, and that he would in that case gladly co-operate with the Commission, all the members of which were known to him. With this indorsement, I took it directly to headquarters, where, at my request, it was copied by Mrs. Frémont, and taken by her to the general's office. He was surrounded by earnest and excited friends, having just received the countermand of his proclamation of conditional emancipation in Missouri; but he examined it, and, after learning that it met the approval of the medical director, he submitted it to the examination of his chief of staff, and then signed it. I have that original copy, in Mrs. Frémont's handwriting, now.

When General Halleck succeeded in command, I took it to him, having first fortified myself by letters from President Lincoln and Secretary Chase, to prevent an immediate veto. He read it, and said that, although he could not have originated such an order, he saw how useful it would be if in good hands, and should not countermand it unless sufficient reason should appear;

ir bread.
from

APPENDIX III.

...ommission could go on with its work under
...der already obtained. From that time forward,
...der General Halleck and all his successors in command, the services of the Commission were freely used.
The funds rapidly increased, and sanitary supplies were
freely distributed wherever needed, from Missouri to
Chattanooga, and far beyond. By the wonderful effi-
ciency of the president, James E. Yeatman, who devoted
his whole time and strength to the work, results were
obtained which would at first have seemed impossible.
The cordial testimony of Generals Grant and Sherman
and Curtis, and many others, was frequently and publicly given to this effect.

It may be that General Frémont overstepped the
limits of army regulations in authorizing the Commission. When the rough draught was prepared, I knew
nothing about such regulations, and know but little
now. But I knew the need of our suffering men, and
the deplorable inadequacy of the means for their relief.
In making provision for such relief under existing exigencies, General Frémont acted under the dictates of
humanity and common sense.

It is my confident opinion, from familiarity with all
the facts at the time, that if his emancipation order had
been equally sustained, notwithstanding its alleged
irregularity, instead of being countermanded with censure, the State of Missouri would have been saved from
more than two years of destructive guerilla warfare.
Even as it was, that order was the first keynote to
the emancipation policy, which soon after prevailed.
Time sets all things right, and honor will ultimately be
given to whom honor is due. The whole administration
of General Frémont in Missouri has been severely criti-

cised. But I anxiously watched it from beginning to end, and after carefully reading the scrutinizing report of the Congressional Committee, the members of which were by no means partial to Frémont, interpreting the testimony by my own knowledge of the facts as they transpired, I would sum up the whole record in a single sentence : Whatever criticism of details may be just, he found Missouri trembling in the balance, between loyalty and secession, with alarming probabilities in the wrong direction ; at the end of three months he left it, although with great difficulties yet to be encountered, as secure to the Union as Massachusetts itself, with slavery already foredoomed. To whom the credit belongs, let impartial history show.

CPSIA information can be obtained
at www.ICGtesting.com
Printed in the USA
BVHW060357150720
583692BV00009B/223